Charities

There are many charities that need financial support and help to continue their work. Therefore, we donate 10% of the net sales of each book to a charity. The charities include: cancer research, diabetes type one, children's hospitals, mental health support and other aid organisations.

Will Jones' Space Adventures and the Money Formula©

By
Christine Thompson-Wells
BA., Dip of Teaching

Illustrations: Brian Platt

If you have purchased this book without its cover, it may be a stolen book. This should be reported to the publisher.

This publication is written and is intended to provide reliable and competent information. Neither the publisher nor the author is under any obligation to provide professional services rendering financial and legal advice or otherwise.

The author and the publisher specifically disclaim any liability that may be incurred from the information within this book.

All rights reserved. No part of this book, including interior design, illustrations, cover design may be reproduced or transmitted in any form by any means (electronic, photocopying, recording or otherwise) without the prior permission of the publisher:

First published 2002 (as 'Rupins')

Copyright© 2005, 2008, 2017 2020

by Christine Thompson-Wells
All rights reserved

Published by Books For Reading On Line.Com

See our website: www.booksforreadingonline.com
or contact us on sales@booksforreadingonline.com

Edited and laid out by John Firth

ISBN 978-0-9551498-6-3

Contents

Chapter One 1
Going for a walk

Chapter Two 17
The visitors from Spectron

Chapter Three 34
Will and Ben meet the King of Spectron

Chapter Four 61
Will meets a Grigan soldier

Chapter Five 75
How Will works with his money

Chapter Six 98
Ben and Will say their farewell to the people of Spectron

Chapter Seven 111
The journey to Ozimoth

Acknowledgements

Thank you to the teachers, head teachers and the students of the participating schools in the Rupins investigation so far:

St Mary's Church of England Primary School, Shinfield, Berkshire;

The Brakenhale School, Bracknell, Berkshire;

Holy Trinity Church of England Primary School, Sunningdale, Surrey;

St Mary's Church of England School, Thatcham, Berkshire;

Compton Primary School, Compton, West Berkshire;

Reading Girls' School, Reading, Berkshire;

and Emma Godfrey.

Author's Note: In the best interest of the story and to keep word harmony some characters' names have changed.

Introduction

This book is written to help children understand the concept of money and how money works in their life.

The story takes place in Ozimoth which is a land of great prosperity.

A spaceship from the planet Spectron comes to Ozimoth and wants to know why this beautiful island in the middle of the sea of Sperra is so successful.

The young reader will find the story stimulating, and yet it does not lose sight of how money can work for the benefit of all.

Chapter One
Going for a walk

Far away on the distant island of Ozimoth, the sun was shining. It was a school day and Will and Millie were just stirring from their sleep. They were about to get out of bed after their mother had called them for the third time.

They had to go to school and neither wanted to get up because they had gone to bed so late the night before. They had been to a school firework display where they had eaten lots of bread, hot potatoes and home-made soup. Millie had eaten her favourite baked bananas and ice cream until she felt her tummy was going to pop.

Like all the children they went to school on the island. The island was very large and their school was a long way from home, which was why they had to get up so soon. Otherwise they would miss the early morning school bus.

Their mum was getting really mad by this time and they heard her coming up the stairs. They could tell that she was mad by the way her footsteps sounded on the stairs! Both children jumped out of bed and almost knocked each other over as they rushed to get ready.

'There you are, it's about time you were both up ...,' she said. 'You're going to miss the bus if you don't hurry.'

If they were quick, they would get to the bus stop on time. It was Friday and the last day of school for the week. It was important to get to school on time today as they had finished their week's homework and they had to hand it in to the teachers. If they were late, there would be trouble!

School was fun, but weekends were even better! At the weekend Will worked for the local farmer.

On Ozimoth, great numbers of grapes were grown. These were sold all over the land and even to other planets and throughout the galaxy. Will's job was to clean all of the trays that were used in washing the grapes. The grapes were kept in rooms that were like huge fridges. He would have to wear a special coat to keep him warm when he worked in these cold rooms.

Now Will had a little mouse called Sniffy: the two were the best of friends. Sniffy loved to stay tucked in Will's pocket and went with him almost everywhere. But when Will was working Sniffy had to stay in Will's bedroom. During these times, Sniffy stayed in Will's old trainer. He seemed to like this smelly old shoe and would sleep there for hours.

Will's sister Millie was a little younger than Will; she too had a little weekend job helping at the local vet's. She loved animals and especially caring for those that were found sick or wounded close to where she lived. The veterinary hospital was close to home, so she could ride to her job on her bike.

Both the children were paid for the work they did. Will would get his money from the farmer after he finished his work on the Sunday. He was paid 5 rupins an hour. This was not a very large amount of money, but it was much more than the pocket money Will got from his parents. Will worked for four hours on a Saturday morning. Every hour meant Will was paid 5 rupins, so on Saturday he got

$$4 \times 5 \text{ rupins} = 20 \text{ rupins}$$

On Sunday he worked for 2 hours so he got

$$2 \times 5 = 10 \text{ rupins}$$

So altogether, he got a total of 30 rupins:

$$20 + 10 = 30 \text{ rupins}$$

He got twice as much for Saturdays as Sundays since he worked twice as long.

Will was a little different from other boys of his age as he had learnt not to spend all of his money when he had earned it; this is what he would do.

After working at the weekend, he would sit on his bed and he would divide his money up into four piles.

While he sat there counting, Sniffy would watch him from Will's pocket.

His piles of money would often look like this:

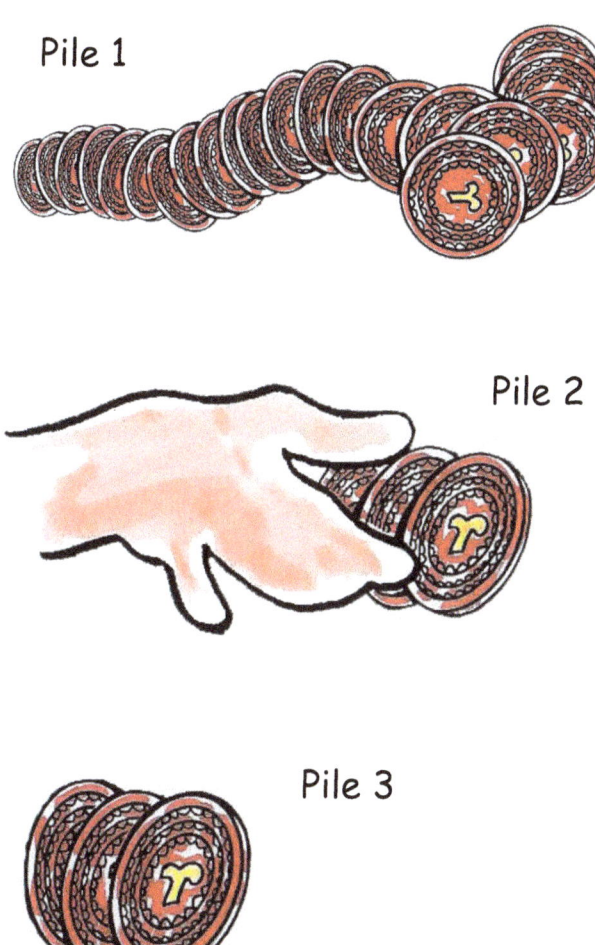

Pile 1

Pile 2

Pile 3

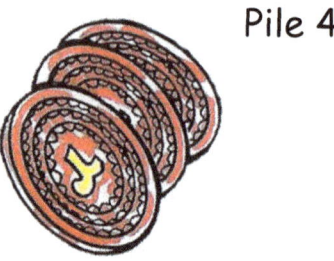

Pile 4

Pile 1 was his SPECIAL money; he used this to buy things he needed for school or for other treats. For instance, sometimes he would buy himself a chocolate and cream pie on the way home from school as a special treat.

Pile 1, this was his SPECIAL money which was 21 rupins.

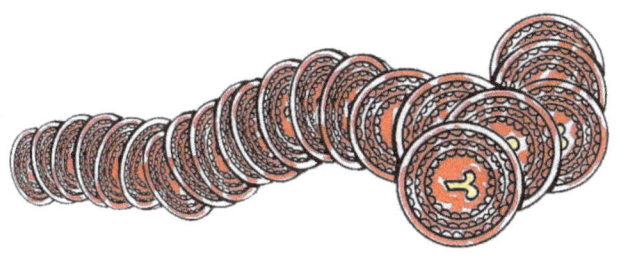

Pile 2, this was his SAVINGS money; he would put 3 rupins into this pile.

Pile 3, this was the money for the CHILDREN'S home. He also put 3 rupins into this pile.

Pile 4 is Will's SECRET pile and he put the remaining 3 rupins into this pile.

It was now Sunday afternoon. Will had finished working and had been paid his 30 rupins. He went up to his room to sort out his money. He was busy doing this when

Millie came home from her job at the vet's. She too had had a very busy day and was tired. She did not sort her money out like her brother; she put all of her money into her piggy bank, which sat beside her bed on the bedside cabinet.

Their mother called up the stairs, 'Could you two wash your hands and get ready for dinner as we are eating early this afternoon.'

Their mother and father were going out for the evening and needed to leave early. They were travelling to Green Hills to visit some friends. The children still had some homework to do and were staying at home to catch up.

After dinner, both Millie and Will did the washing and drying of the dishes, put them away and then Will went back upstairs to continue sorting out his money.

Sniffy was asleep in the trainer when Will went back into his room; the money was on his bed as he had left it. He placed his 3 rupins into his savings book and the 21 rupins were put into his pocket; the third amount he put into an envelope for the children's home. He liked to give the

children's home a little of his money. He knew that, though Ozimoth was very prosperous, the children in the home had no parents, which was sad. Will was thankful to have his parents and knew he and his sister were very fortunate.
The fourth pile of rupins was for his secret place and project.

By now Sniffy was awake so Will picked him up, put him into his shirt pocket and went downstairs.

The children's parents had said good-bye and reminded them not to forget their homework.

Millie was busy watching television when Will came down, 'Aren't you supposed to be doing your homework?' he asked. She replied, 'Aren't you?' 'I'm doing it later.' said Will.

With Sniffy securely in his pocket, he went outside and decided to take a walk. It was a lovely afternoon and too nice to be indoors.

Chapter Two
The visitors from Spectron

Will was enjoying his walk when he met his friend Ben. Ben lived on the other side of town and he and Will had not seen each other for a very long time. Ben had his skateboard with him and had just finished skateboarding when they met.

Ozimoth was a nice place to live. The people were very friendly and there were lots of trees and flowers everywhere.

Another great thing was living so close to the beach. Being so close to the sea the children would go swimming every day after school before doing their homework.

The two boys chatted as they walked along the seafront road.

It was now getting dark; they had been so busy telling each other their latest news that they had not realised how late it had become.

They had just walked past the mangroves and the moon was now showing in the sky. Will could even see some stars. He thought, 'it's getting really late!' Will said to Ben, 'I think we had better head home, it's really late now.' Ben nodded and said, 'I think you're right.'

It was just at that moment they heard a whirring sound in the sky above them. Both boys looked up and saw a huge black shape hovering right above their heads. Ben grabbed Will's arm in fear and both boys started to shake.

Lights were flashing over their heads and the whirring sound grew louder. Ben said in a trembly voice 'What is that?' Will replied, 'I think it's a spaceship...'

'What's it doing here then?' was Ben's reply. Will replied, 'I don't know but I do know we had better get out of here in a hurry.'

Just then the whirring stopped, and the spaceship landed on the road, right in front of them. Both boys could not move. Sniffy was still in Will's pocket. Will knew that Sniffy was also scared and that things were very wrong.

As the boys watched, the door of the spaceship opened. Walking slowly out through the doorway they saw some space people from the planet of Spectron. The boys knew about these people because they had visited Ozimoth before.

'They are fighters and take hostages,' Will thought. They were known to be angry and hostile people.
Ben looked on. Will felt Ben trembling beside him, 'What do you think they want?' Ben whispered. Will, said, 'I don't know...' Both boys were panic-stricken and could not move.

All this time, the bright blue lights from the spaceship continued to spin around.

A very tall space man, who looked like the Leader, walked towards the two boys and spoke in a different language. Ben and Will looked at each other, not knowing what was being said to them. The Leader appeared to become agitated because the boys did not understand him.

At that moment, some headlights from a vehicle appeared over the hill in the far distance. The Space Leader saw the lights. Before Ben and Will could make a run for it, they mysteriously found themselves inside the spaceship. Sniffy was still cowering in Will's pocket. Will stroked him softly and said, 'Don't worry Sniff, we will be out of here before you know it...'

A boy of about their own age showed the boys into a large hall within the spaceship. Ben said, 'This is just like the hall at school...' They were then told to sit down by the young space boy. The language the boy used was very different from that spoken on Ozimoth but both Will and Ben seemed to understand somehow what was being said to them.

Suddenly all sorts of things started to happen inside the spaceship. Tables came up out of the floor and seats emerged from the walls. Down from the ceiling of the spaceship came a board operated by computer-type buttons which were flashing down its side. Will was so amazed he forgot to feel afraid. He found it very difficult to sit still and just wait for the next thing to happen!

The space boy watched as Will walked around the hall touching the walls, which were made of a type of stainless steel, dotted about with orange lights. These lights somehow reflected through the steel of all of the walls, which he found fascinating – he did metal work at school and had used some stainless steel in a school project.

Will moved closer to the space boy to have a better look at him. 'He looks very different from the boys at school,' Will thought.

Suddenly the whirring motor sounds started to get louder and there was a jolt within the whole spaceship. Will had the sensation that the spaceship was moving at a great speed.

Ben was still sitting on one of the stainlesssteel seats; he was starting to look very frightened and was indeed very nervous.

Will moved from looking at the space boy and went over to stand close to his friend. Will said to him, 'Don't worry, I think we will be alright. This boy seems to be friendly.' Will gave Sniffy another little stroke to try to reassure him too.

Standing there in the spaceship, Will wondered where they were going to be taken. He suddenly thought of the rupins that he had put into his pocket while he was in his bedroom. He felt for them and they were still in the pocket of his jeans, just as he had left them.

The spaceship continued to travel at what seemed to be a very great speed. Will had realised that the whirring sound had gone into a steady hum.

After a short while, the space boy pointed to what appeared to be windows emerging from behind the walls of the spaceship. The boy moved over to one of the windows and made a sign for both Ben and Will to look out with him. Ben and Will peered out and saw so many coloured planets and stars that they knew they were going to another galaxy.

Now that Ozimoth was trading produce with other galaxies, more and more stars and planets were becoming known and more discoveries were being made about other people and how they lived.

Spectron, however, where this particular spaceship came from, was not considered to be one of the friendly planets.

As the boys stared through the window at the passing stars and planets, the Space

Elder came back into the room with some boys and girls of Will and Ben's age.

The space boy, who had been waiting with Will and Ben, went to the board that had come down from the ceiling and started to push some buttons. 'It is like a mixture of the computer screen at home and the whiteboard that my teacher uses at school...' Will thought.

The space boy started to show Ben and Will scenes from around where they lived on Ozimoth. There on the screen, they saw the boats at the boat ramp; this was where Will's dad went out fishing for crabs and lobsters. Ben then recognised his own home.

Both boys looked at each other. Will could see that Ben had started to become more and more puzzled and even more nervous than before.

The spaceship was going faster. The space boy signalled to Will to move over and stand next to him near the screen.
Some of the group of space children sat down on the floor while others sat on the seats that had come out of the walls.

'What did the space boy want?' Will wondered...

Chapter Three
Will and Ben meet the King of Spectron

Will went to stand next to the space boy and as he did so he suddenly saw the shadow of a smile come across his face. Ben stayed glued to the seat where he had been the whole time. He still seemed very scared. 'Nothing is going to move Ben from that seat!' Will thought.

Some of the space children moved closer to Ben. Will could see by the expression on his friend's face that he felt a little uncomfortable at this but he could not really do very much about it!

The skin of the space children was a light golden-brown colour. The girls wore a type of dress which reminded Ben of his history books. They looked something like those girls from early Roman times but, at the same time, strangely different. The boys had the same colour skin, but their hair was cut in a way that Ben had never seen before. It was very short at the front and pointed down at the back. 'Strange!' he thought.

The space boys wore a light-coloured tunic. Ben thought, 'I wouldn't like to wear that!'

Ben realised both boys had not said very much to each other since the space ship had picked them up on the road by the sea. Will seemed to be muttering something. Ben was not close enough to hear him.

More and more pictures of the areas where the boys lived came up on to the screen. There was suddenly a picture of Millie. Will felt very sad when he thought about her and started to worry. She was in the house by herself and his mother had told him, 'Do not leave your sister alone.' He now felt a pang of anguish in his stomach with this thought!

Even more pictures were shown on the screen, pictures of the farm where Will worked and then a picture of Will cleaning some wire boards at the farm. Even Ben was surprised at this! He looked at Will and saw the puzzled expression on his friend's face.

Will suddenly realised – he had been explaining to the space children and to Ben all there was to know about the pictures they were seeing on the screen. Up until this time, he hadn't realised he had been telling the space children all about his life at home.

He was completely bewildered as to why any space people should be interested in him and what he did!

The whirring of the spaceship was slowing down and Will could see more lights through the spaceship windows. These lights were bright green. He thought, 'The space ship must be about to land.' He was right. The next thing was that the ship stopped. There were some clunking sounds and the children got up and stood quietly. Then in a very orderly fashion they walked out of a door that opened from within the wall of the spacecraft. The door closed after the last of the space children had left the ship.

Ben and Will were left in the hall alone. Will sat next to his friend. Sniffy was still firmly in Will's pocket. Will could feel Sniffy's body relaxing a little now.

Perhaps he sensed things were not so dangerous. Ben started to say, 'What do you think of...?' when the door suddenly opened again. It was the Space Elder. He made a sign for the boys to follow him, and they did as he bade.

The boys followed the Space Elder through long corridors lit with brightly orange coloured lights. The place had a friendly feel about it. Will was expecting to feel frightened, but he did not in any way. Like Sniffy, he felt more relaxed now.

The corridors were large and oval in shape and appeared to be made out of the same stainless steel material that the spaceship was made from.

They walked through so many corridors that Will felt sure they would never find their way back again.

At last they stopped and there before them was Spectron. A place so beautiful that Ben thought he must be dreaming. Will could also not believe what he was seeing! He gasped at the sight! In the centre was a magnificent white building.

There were palm-type trees and running rivers, and other equally beautiful buildings. 'It all seems lovely, magical and peaceful...' Will thought.

This was nothing like the image of Spectron that his world knew about. The images they knew were of a dry and barren land without any beautiful buildings. He was not aware that Spectron would have such magnificent rivers and large green trees.

Both boys were taken to a building, not to the one they had seen at first, but to another building that appeared to be at the end of a long road. This building had many children of all ages playing in it. The children were speaking the same language as Ben and Will and so they could understand what the children were saying.

Will thought to himself, 'Have these children been taken away like us?' There were no space children to be seen. Not, at least, any children that looked like the ones on the spaceship.

This building was magnificent, shining, and green. The Space Elder led the boys to a great chamber within the building. He pointed to some chairs for them to sit on. Both boys sat down. They waited, wondering what was going to happen. Ben said to Will, 'I'm getting really hungry. I wonder if we can get something to eat?' Will shrugged his shoulders; he could not see any shops around, so he supposed that, perhaps, these people did not eat.

As if the Space Elder had read their minds he appeared with a tray of food. On the tray were grapes; Will recognised the grapes; they were like the ones the farmer grew at home. There were two buns with meat that resembled beef burgers and cheese, and two glasses of pink fizzy foam. When Will tasted the pink foam, he said to Ben, 'Try this, it's really good. It's like a strawberry milk shake that we have at home.'

Seeing the food, Will too realised how hungry he was. Both boys ate and were almost finished when the space boy from the ship arrived. Will was finishing his drink, which he was really enjoying, when the boy started to talk to them. The boy was not opening his mouth, but he must be using mental telepathy, Will thought.

Will was thinking 'Why had the people from the planet Spectron been considered to be hostile people?' Will had not asked the question, but the boy went on to answer this very question. Will was amazed and thought, 'I will have to be very careful what I think about in the future...'

Ben then said to the space boy, 'Why have you brought us here?'
The space boy told both boys that now a new King had taken over Spectron they

were going through a time of change. They were very sad about the pain and suffering they had caused in the past and did not want to ever go through that time again.

The boy continued to speak, 'Not all of his people felt as the new King did and there were people who wanted to fight in wars, but while their new King was on the throne, they were going to try to build a good future.' The new King had many ideas about what their planet could offer to other galaxies and planets and wanted to promote trade between each of them.

All of the time the Space Elder stood listening to the conversation between the boys. He then started to nod his head. Just then, everything went very quiet. The great doors opened and a very young and handsome man walked through them and over to the boys. The space boy said, 'This is our King and he would like to talk to you.'

Will could not believe that he was standing before a King. The King looked at both boys and Will saw what he thought was a kind of smile on the Space King's face.

The King's skin was the same colour as the space children's but his hair was a rich bright gold colour Will had never seen before.

He wore silken robes and had a gold band around his head: this had a very large green stone in it.

Will thought 'That must be a sort of emerald or something like it.'

The Space Elder left the boys alone with the King. The King started to speak to the boys, firstly by mental telepathy and then words started to come out from his mouth in the same language as Ben and Will spoke. Before both boys realised, they were talking to the King and explaining their ways and how they did things at home.

The King was very interested. He asked Will, 'How do you trade in Ozimoth? How do you use your money?' Will brought out his rupins from inside his pocket and held them in his hand. All of this time Sniffy had made no movement.

Will and Ben were led, by the King, to a table that was in the corner of the great chamber. The King asked Will to show him the money and was told to 'put it on to the table....' Will did this. The King asked, 'What is the money called and how much do you have there?' Will explained that each coin was called a rupin and that he had earned this money through working on a grape-growing farm for a farmer. He went on to explain: 'I work at the weekend and work for 6 hours.

'I work for 4 hours on a Saturday morning and for 2 hours on a Sunday morning. I do odd jobs to help the farmer, which helps him and he pays me for my help.'

The King asked, 'How much do you get paid?' Will explained, 'I get 5 rupins an hour.' Will was becoming more than interested in this whole conversation: 'Why should a King,be interested in a boy who earns 5 rupins an hour?'

Just then, the door opened and the Space Elder came back in, in a hurry. The Elder ushered the King away from the boys and spoke quietly to him. Will thought the King looked very concerned by what the Elder was telling him.

The King came back to the boys and said, 'I will talk with you later; but now I have something to do.'

The Space Elder directed all three boys out of the chamber and down some corridors. All of the space children now followed them. Ben quickly looked around and there were hundreds of children. He could not help thinking how nice they all seemed to be. They were busily chatting to each other in their own language, which he did not understand. They were not communicating with him in any way. He thought 'They were not trying to communicate with me; this is why I cannot understand the language.'

They were moving very quickly down long corridors now and they seemed to be going deeper and deeper down into the building. 'This building,' Will thought, 'went on forever.'

The corridors had the same orange lights showing them the way as he had seen when they first arrived on Spectron. 'The green lights', he thought 'are only on the outside of the buildings.'

The Elder and the young space boy were leading all of them down into what Will thought must be a safety or secret area. Eventually they were shown out of the corridor into what seemed like a large open area. They had arrived. They were deep, deep down in the centre of Spectron. They saw a large open area; it even had a very large lake in the centre. Will realised he could not see the other side of the lake. 'There are trees and birds and clouds; it all looks so similar to Ozimoth,' he thought. Suddenly he thought of his friend Ben. 'Where is he?' he wondered!

Ben had lagged behind; Will looking around for his friend spotted Ben way back, standing within the group of space children. He was communicating with them. He had made friends with the children. 'They are telling him what is going on, on the surface of Spectron,' Will thought.

This aroused Will's interest. He made his way through the crowd of space children to talk to Ben and the group he had made friends with. Ben started to tell Will what he had learned. The planet of Spectron was being invaded by the Grigans.

The Grigans lived in a galaxy that was far, far away and it had taken this band of attackers many light years to reach Spectron. The children had been brought down here so that they would not get hurt if there was a battle or war.

Will saw the children he had seen when they arrived at the building. They were the ones who looked like Ben and himself. They were not space children, but they were speaking and playing with the space children. They seemed to be very happy.

Ben told Will, 'The King is going to try to communicate with the Grigans and try to avoid an attack...'

Will suddenly realised he had left his rupins on the table in the corner of the great chamber.

He told Ben, 'I won't be long; I've left my money in the great chamber.' Before Ben could say anything, Will was running back up the corridor. As he ran, he thought, 'I hope I find the great chamber and my rupins.'

He was running like the wind, through corridor after corridor, passing many orange lights, all of the time going upwards and upwards!

Chapter Four
Will meets a Grigan soldier

Corridor after orange-lit corridor he ran through; he could hear sounds coming from above. He had not heard anything like it before. He put his hand down and Sniffy was curled up in a ball in his pocket. Will gave him a little pat to reassure him that he was safe.

Will at last saw the familiar doorway to the great chamber; he again heard strange sounds. This time he knew that they were coming from inside the chamber.

Slowly he made his way nearer. Will stood at the entrance of the great chamber just behind the doorway. If he stretched his neck, he could just see what was happening!

He saw the King sitting on a magnificent throne! He could not recall having seen this throne before. The King was wearing battle dress and looked ready for war. Standing before the King was a very large male shape. This shape was also dressed in a type of battle armour.

Standing around the throne were other Spectron Elders and Leaders; they too, were dressed ready for battle. 'They all look similar to the Space Elder we met when we were first taken away in the spacecraft,' he thought.

Suddenly, he felt something very large and cold grasping him by the back of his neck. He turned and he looked straight into the face of a Grigan soldier! He could not make the man's eyes out because he was covered from head to toe in a type of battle dress. The man was obviously looking down at him though and one small movement of the man's arm moved Will forward towards the King and the Leader of the Grigans.

As the two moved forward, Will could not feel his feet walking; instead he felt his feet sliding over the very shiny surface of the floor.

The King looked at Will as the two crossed the floor in the great chamber.

The soldier's footsteps and battle dress made a clamour as they moved.

The soldier's hold on the back of Will's neck was so strong that Will started to feel light-headed and not really able to concentrate.

The Grigan Leader made a sign and the soldier released his grip on Will's neck. Will thought that he was going to fall down. One of the Spectron Elders saw what was going to happen and he moved swiftly to catch Will.

The Spectron Elder stayed by Will's side until he could stand steadily by himself. The Elder then went back to join the rest of the Elders and Leaders at the side of the King's throne.

The King and the Grigan Leader were in conversation.

Will slowly started to collect himself and began to feel a little better. As he stood there in the great chamber, he realised to his surprise that he could understand what the King and the Grigan Leader were discussing.

He did not know how this was happening. The language they were speaking was so different from his. He stood motionless for a long time watching the leaders. He now realised that he was using telepathy.

By Will concentrating on the sounds that the leaders were making, his mind had the ability to understand their different languages and what they were talking about.

The Grigans had always been a warring nation and they had come to Spectron to attack it and take its wealth. However, the King had started to talk to the Grigan Leader and to explain his good intentions for his people and for the planet of Spectron.

The Grigan Leader appeared to be interested in what the King had to say. Will learned that the Grigans had completely surrounded the planet of Spectron and that by now, there should be a full-scale war going on. However, that was not happening.

The King informed the Grigan Leader, 'I am willing to fight to save our planet...' and continued to explain to the Grigan Leader, 'not all of my people want peace and some do want to fight you.'

The Grigan Leader told the King, 'Some of your fighters have already attacked us; we do not know their fate...'

Will knew he had been standing in the great chamber for a long time witnessing these two Leaders communicating. He then remembered why he had come to the great chamber, to pick up his rupins from the table.

Will thought nobody was really looking at him, so he would make his way to the table to pick up his money. Just as he started to move, the soldier again grabbed him by the back of the neck. This time the hold seemed even stronger. Will's body started to go limp and heavy and a feeling of darkness started to fill his mind.

Just at that moment, the King spoke to Will and the soldier released his grip on the back of Will's neck.

The King asked, 'What were you moving for and where were you going?' Will explained, through speaking, 'I came back here to pick up my money which I had left on the table in the corner over there...' He pointed in the direction of the table.

If he squinted, he could just make out the money sitting on the table; the chamber was so large that the table appeared to be a long way from him.

Will's heart was still racing; the soldier's grip had hurt, and he was still feeling the soreness on his neck.

The King stood up from his throne; both the King and the Grigan Leader walked purposely towards Will.

Will started to feel nervous. He wondered what was going to happen.

Just as Will was wondering this, more Grigans in battle dress suddenly entered through the large door. They kept on coming until a crowd stood all around the chamber. Will could not make out any faces; they all looked the same.

The King and the Grigan Leader were now standing beside Will. The King spoke and said, 'We will go to the table to see your money.'

The three walked towards the large table in the corner of the great chamber. Will felt very strange, as he knew that all of these different people were watching him.

Chapter Five
How Will works with his money

He was there, at the edge of the table looking down at his money; it was just as he had left it.

The King spoke with Will and asked, 'How do you use this money, in your land?' Will replied, 'I use this money to buy the things I need.' Will continued speaking in a loud clear voice and explained: 'I work for a farmer.'

Will told the leaders about the cows and how they produced milk which people used for drinking and making milkshakes. He also explained about the corn and maize that the farmer grew in the fields. 'My mother makes bread and biscuits from these and they taste very good,' he said The Grigan Leader seemed to be showing a great interest in what Will was saying now. Will was surprised. The Grigan hadn't seemed interested before.

The Grigan Leader then said, in a deep and muffled voice. 'We have much land on the planet of Grigan and it could be used;

we do not know anything about farming and growing things.' Both leaders were showing a lot of interest in this other way of life.

Will then picked up his money and handed one rupin to the King and one to the Grigan. Will explained, 'I earn this money and use it to buy all sorts of things.' He looked down at his old trainers. 'For instance, I will need to buy some new trainers in a couple of weeks.' Both the King and the Grigan Leader looked at the trainers he was wearing. They were old and battered, almost as old as the one that was used as Sniffy's bed.

Both the Grigan Leader and the King seemed to find Will's old trainers funny. Will could not see the funny side at all! The King now asked Will, 'How do you get this money?'

'I work on a Saturday and Sunday and the farmer pays me 5 rupins an hour. I do not go to school on a Saturday or Sunday, so I use that time to earn some money for myself. I usually earn about 30 rupins for the work I do at the weekend.'

Will continued to explain, 'I put 21 rupins in my pocket, which I use to buy the special things I need, and I put 3 rupins into my savings account. I give 3 rupins to my friends at the children's home who are not as fortunate as me and I put 3 into my secret place.'

The King again said to him, 'Show me with the money here how you do this...?' By now, several of the other Grigans and

Spectron Elders had gathered around the Leaders, Will, the table and money.

Will looked at the 21 rupins on the table He put his hand out to move the money around to show all of the space people and the Leaders how he worked out his money each week after the farmer had paid him.

'When I have finished working on a Sunday, I go home and I divide my money up into separate piles. This way I know that I will always have enough money for each purpose (my own use, the children's home, my savings and my secret pile) and I will not run out.'

He also explained, 'At school we learn to divide money like this in the mathematics class.'

He explained, 'I divide my money into four piles.' He then moved the rupins into 4 different piles. One pile had 12 rupins, and then he made three piles with 3 rupins in each.

He explained: 'Pile 1 is my SPECIAL money, and has 12 rupins in it.'

'Pile 2 is my SAVINGS money and looks like this...'

'Pile 3 is the money I give to the CHILDREN'S home in our town....'

'and Pile 4 is my SECRET money.' The King and the Grigan Leader appeared to be intrigued at this. The Grigan Leader repeated 'My secret money?' Will nodded his head in reply but said nothing.

Will now pointed to the four separate piles of money on the table.

The King too was curious – he asked Will, 'What is your secret money?' Will thought about this question for a while before he answered the King and the Grigan Leader. Will quickly glanced at the Grigan Leader; Will could see that he too was waiting for an answer.

Will had never told anybody about his secret money. He knew now that he did not have much choice! If he didn't tell, he did not know what would happen.

He started to explain, 'Well, my secret money is for something that I want to do in the future. I collect old coins and stamps from other planets and galaxies. Sometimes I sell some of these at our local fairs and markets to make a profit. With the extra money I make from selling these coins and stamps I can buy more coins and stamps or save the extra money. If I buy extra stamps and coins, I am adding to my collection.

'When I have earned extra rupins from selling my stamps and coins I sometimes put this money into my savings account.

'I do put my secret money into an account that gives me some extra money for saving it. This money I will use for me as I would like to be a writer or an inventor and I know that one day I will need that money. Once I have put that money into the account, I do not ever take it out until the right time comes and that is when I really, really need it.'

The King and the Grigan Leader looked at each other. Then the King said, 'And what do you do with your savings?' Will replied: 'I keep that to spend some, not all of it, on holidays and if I need to buy anything special for the family. For instance, when it's my sister Millie's birthday, as I like to buy her a nice birthday present. But I am careful not to just spend it without a lot of thought!' The King said, 'And will you get some new boots for yourself with your special money?'

Will again, looked down at his old trainers; he replied, 'I might!'

By this time there were a great number of space people interested in what was going on around the table and they all did seem to be standing very close to the King, the Grigan Leader and Will.

The King spoke to one of the senior Elders, to ask him to take Will back down to the other children.

The King then said to Will, 'Leave the money on the table.' Will did what he was told.

Will followed the Space Elder down the passageways and once again through the orange-lit corridors. Will could not help thinking 'I hope I get my rupins back. I really do need to buy a new pair of trainers.' The Elder answered him, 'You will get your money back when you leave... Our King and the Grigan Leader want to talk about how they can use the information you have given them to give us a better future. Our King was very impressed with the way you work with your money and that you will not allow yourself to run out.'

Will felt surprised and pleased when he heard this.

'We were once a planet of great prosperity but, because we did not work with our wealth, we lost it. We now have to find a way to recover and to build a future for ourselves and for our children,' said the Space Elder.

Will thought about the words that had just been communicated to him and he decided that he liked these people.

The Elder and Will joined the other children. Ben saw Will come through the great opening and ran to his friend.

'Where have you been?' Ben asked, 'Boy have I been worried about you!' he said.

Will explained about all that had happened up in the great chamber and how he had met the fierce Leader from the planet Grigan. Because the children had walked deep, deep down into the middle of the planet of Spectron, they knew nothing of what was going on, on the surface between the Grigans and the Spectron people.

By this time, what appeared to be a beautiful sunset could be seen far across the lake. Some of the space children were playing on the sandy shores of the lake. They were playing ball and Will was sure he could hear them laughing. However, it was a different kind of laugh from what he was used to.

Large tables suddenly came up from under the ground. All of the children ran across to them. People were now laying the tables with all types of delicious-looking foods.

The boys noticed there were women there. It was the first time they had seen space women. The women had the same coloured skin as the children and wore flowing tunics. They had flowers in their hair and wore gold bracelets on their arms and ankles.

'They look very different from the clothes my mother and sister wear...' Will thought.

One woman offered the boys some food. Both took a type of clear, transparent plate from the pile of plates on the table. The space woman then filled the plate to overflowing! There was fruit and a flat food that resembled pizza, breads and other foods that Will had not seen before.

Both Will and Ben sat down on the sandy shore and ate all of the food on their space plates. They now felt much better and hadn't realised how hungry they had become, since their last meal.

This was the first time that Sniffy had put his head out of Will's pocket. Will took a little of the food and gave it to his pet. The Space Elder was watching the two boys and he seemed to approve when he saw what Will was doing.

Sniffy was as hungry as the boys and ate everything that Will gave to him.

Once they had eaten, an Elder came to walk with the boys back to the King who was now sitting on his throne with the Leader of the Grigans standing at his side.

Chapter Six
Ben and Will say their farewell to the People of Spectron

The boys entered the great chamber and Ben stopped in his tracks as he saw the King sitting on his large and grand throne. Will pulled at his sweater sleeve and said, 'Don't stop, keep walking. Don't you know it's disrespectful to stop walking when you are supposed to be going to meet a King?' Ben was speechless as he made his way towards the King, his Leaders and Elders.

The King stood up from his throne and spoke to both Ben and Will. 'We would like to thank you for showing us the way you use your money. I know that our Elder has told you that we were once a great and prosperous nation. However, we ran out of money and our people and our land have suffered.

'Because we were foolish and we spent all of our money as we earned it, we had very little money left if a crisis came to the planet.

'So, when a crisis came to our planet, Spectron, we were unable to cope with the problems that came with it. We could not rebuild our nation, our soldiers did not have any food and we could not pay them any wages. Through this time, our children were not being educated and they now have to catch up. They did not have the good food, which you see this moon. We must not let that happen in the future.

'We have slowly started to rebuild Spectron but we still have a great deal of work to do.

'Warring space invaders attacked us and then we went out and attacked other galaxies to get money and goods. This created more wars. None of our actions has helped us nor have they done us any good. We have to change. If we did not change, there would not be a very good or fair future for our children.'

At this point, the Grigan Leader too started to communicate with Ben and Will. 'I would like to know even more about your continent and your planet and the way you live. I do know that you send food to other planets and galaxies and that, one moon, we would like to have some of your food on the planet of Grigan.'

The King signalled to the Elder who had brought the boys from deep down in the corridors. The King then communicated. 'You will be taken back to your planet and your continent; you will be taken to your homes...'

Ben and Will both said 'Thank you.' They turned and walked out of the great chamber behind the Spectron Space Elder.

As they got to the doorway, they were aware that all of the children too had come up from down by the edge of the lake. They were there to see them return to the spaceship and to communicate their goodbyes. All of the children were waving as Ben and Will left the great chamber.

Back in the great chamber the King and the Grigan Leader set about to form a money system that would allow the two planets to grow food and buy goods and produce from each other.

The King said to the Grigan Leader, 'If our people are so busy growing and making things and also becoming prosperous, they will not want to fight because both of our peoples will have enough food and they will not want to take wealth or food from other planets and galaxies.'

The King then called his court together and told them, 'We are now going to devise a plan that will work for all of the people of Spectron. I will form a Government and a Treasury. We will work together to create an ideal planet Spectron. The money of Spectron will be used to secure our future and it will work this way.'

The King ordered some piles of money to be brought from the deep underground vaults.

'Our money will be put into four piles and this is how it will work. We will use Will's idea to begin with. The first pile of money is our Special Money; we will use this for rebuilding and other major planet works that need to be done.

'With this special money, we will provide hospitals, education, parks, highways and roads and develop banks which will be run by the government. The developing banks will help to support our farmers who will grow all types of grains. We will grow more grain than we need. This will be a surplus. After all of our people have had enough, we will use the surplus, extra grains for trading with other planets and galaxies.

'The second pile is our Responsible pile.

 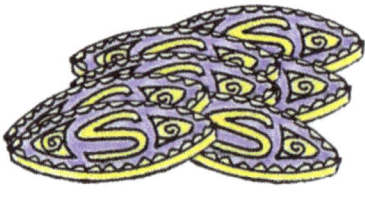 

'This pile is for our people and is to help people who cannot work as they used to. It will also be used for our children whose parents have died in the wars and for those people who are disadvantaged at this present time while we are rebuilding our nation.

'Our third pile of money is our Trade Money. Will called this his Secret Money and this will be used to build up trade and to trade with other galaxies and worlds or planets. Then all the planets and galaxies will be helping each other. We will buy things like grapes from Ozimoth. They will use their trade money to buy our grain.

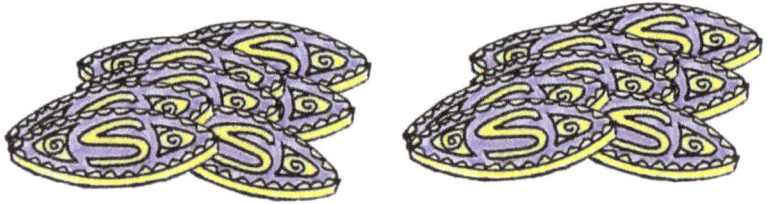

'This way we will start to build our future. We will meet other people and trade our goods so we have all our people need.
'The last pile is our fourth pile and will be used for our future prosperity.

'This last pile is our savings. This money is the money we keep in our vaults. This will be used to give us security which will allow us to develop in the future and to help in times of need.'

The King then pointed to the fourth pile of money.

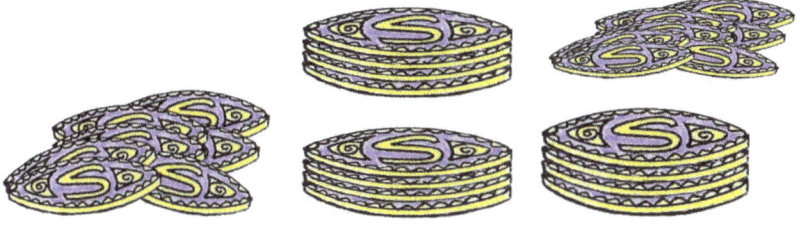

'This will provide security for us, and our children. It will help us to build up to the prosperity that was once enjoyed by the people of Spectron.'

He then spoke to the Government Ministers.

'All of the people who want to and are able to work will be paid for their labour. They will be paid with money and they can then buy what they need.'

The Grigan Leader and his senior soldiers agreed that this was a good and fair way to use the money and that they would be doing the same with their money once they were back on the planet Grigan.

Chapter Seven
The journey to Ozimoth

Ben and Will were now back on the spaceship where the space boy was waiting for them. He handed Will the rupins which had been left on the table in the great chamber.

The space boy started to speak to the boys in their language. Both Ben and Will were now used to communicating with him through telepathy.

Will asked the boy, 'How old are you?' and the boy replied 'Four thousand, seven hundred and forty-five moons.' That took Will a while to work out in years, but somehow he did.

'What is your name?' Ben asked. The boy replied, 'Kii'. Ben, exclaimed, 'That's a different name!'

Will wanted to know more about him so he asked, 'Where do you go to school? Who are your parents? Why did Spectron have such a difficult and warring past?' Both boys started asking questions at the same time.

Kii said, 'One question at a time! First, I go to school with the other children. We have a special building, which you have not seen yet. Your second question is about my parents. My father is the King you were speaking to!' Will could feel his mouth drop open, and then said, 'You mean you are a prince?' Kii replied, 'I suppose I must be but I do not see myself as a prince. I just know that, one day, I may be elected as the King of Spectron and, if this is so, I need to know as much as possible about money and how it works on other planets.'

The familiar whirring of the spaceship motors became more intense and Will knew that he and Ben were on their way back home.

Kii started to talk again. Will thought to himself, 'Kii is thinking about the questions we have asked him.'

'You wanted to know why we had such a warring past? Before my father became the King my great uncle's son was the King. He was a very good King, but he had an army that overtook his power and a General was put into his place. This King died as a prisoner. While the generals were in control, all we had were wars. The generals did not know anything about money and trading, and this is what my father is now trying to put right. He wants to repair the damage that has been done to our people and to our prosperity. This is why it has been so good for me to get to know you and to understand why you work and what you do with your money when you have earned it...'

The motors of the spaceship started to slow down. Both Ben and Will ran to the windows. Through the night sky and clouds, Will saw his home in the moonlight.

The spaceship did not stop at Will's home, but it travelled to Ben's home where it hovered over the front garden. It came down low enough for Ben to walk out of the ship easily and on to his garden path. Will and Kii watched him go in through the front door. Ben turned and waved to them both and shouted, 'Hope to see you again, Kii.' He then closed the door behind him.

The next time the spaceship slowed down it was at Will's home. Will's home had a very large garden so it could easily come close enough to the house without Will having to walk any distance at all. The ship was so close to the back door that it would take him about one step, and he would be in the house.

Will was about to leave the spaceship, but he felt very sad deep down within his stomach. He had come to like Kii a lot and would like to see him in the future. Kii replied, 'We will meet again as I too like you and I would like you to visit Spectron in the future.'

The Space Elder too came to Will to say, goodbye. The Elder said, 'Do take good care of your mouse; he is a very good friend.' Will stroked his friend Sniffy who was still safely inside his pocket.

Will left the spaceship and went into his home. When Will turned around and looked back to wave all he could see was a disappearing bright blue light that was moving so quickly it was out of sight in a blink.

Millie was still watching television as he went into the lounge. She said, 'I thought you were going out for a walk'.

Millie hadn't missed Will. No time seemed to have passed at all.

Will wasn't really aware of where the time had gone; he thought he had left the house many hours previously but if his sister had not even missed him, perhaps he must have just had a dream about what had happened. He thought about all of the experiences. He had been walking along with Ben on the seafront road when they first encountered the spaceship. 'Where had that time gone to?' he wondered.
He went to his room and put Sniffy into his trainer, then sat on the bed. His other

rupins were still as he had left them. He felt inside his pocket and brought out his money. He counted it, '19, 20, 21 rupins. Yes, it's all still here,' he thought.

He placed all of the money out on the bed cover and then started saying to himself:

'Pile 1, is my SPECIAL pile and is 21 rupins.
'Pile 2, is my SAVINGS pile and is 3 rupins.
'Pile 3 is my CHILDREN'S pile and is 3 rupins.
'Pile 4 is my SECRET pile and is 3 rupins.

'This makes 30 rupins and is the money I have earned working for the farmer.'
All of his money was exactly as it was before the adventure.

He put it away into a safe place and went downstairs to join his sister to watch television.

As he came in through the door, she was eating ice cream and she said, 'Would you like some ice cream, Will?' He still felt full and said, 'I think I've had enough to eat at the moment, thanks...'

He thought, 'I do feel really full, I suppose Spectron and Kii must have been real!'

As time went on, he started to believe that he had just imagined the whole episode on Spectron.

Will and Ben met several weeks later but neither of them could talk about the visit to Spectron or the adventure at first. Then Ben said, 'Did we really go to Spectron?' Will felt relieved and replied, 'I think we did.'

The boys had met on the seafront road, just where the spaceship had landed. However, there were no spaceships to be seen now!

It was several months later, when Will was working for the farmer that he thought he heard the whirring of a spaceship's motor. He looked up and Kii was waving to him; he knew now that he had not imagined anything and that it had been a real experience in his life.

He longed for the day when once again he could travel with his friend Kii in the spaceship and meet up with everyone he had encountered on Spectron.

'I do hope my money system is working for them too,' he thought happily to himself.

Comments from readers

By Emma Selwood

This is a very well written book. I very much like the language the author uses. It's not too hard to be understood and not so easy as to be boring. The book never gets dull, it is always exciting. I just want to turn the page. I would recommend this book for ages six to ten years. This is a very exciting and adventurous book.

By Julia Cushion – aged 8

I think the story is very well described and it makes me feel like I'm in the book. I think I can see everything that is happening.

Rupins are money that they get in Ozimoth and I think it's about equal to to five pence in UK money.

I think the writer has made it feel very real and hasn't just made it up. She makes you feel like you are there.

The main characters were the King, the person from the other planet Grigan and Ben and Will. Will was a very caring boy as he gave part of the money he earned to the children in the home who were not as fortunate as him.

I think the writer has done a great job of making everything clear so you can understand it. If I could change one thing I would probably put a few less characters in it.

Rupins has been scientifically trialed in five schools in Berkshire and Surrey, England. Following are some of the comments made by the children within the trial.

Elizabeth Schogidd

I think that *Rupins* was a very good book, I liked the story. I think it will help me in the future. I will put my money in the four piles from now on. I think the story was very interesting and will help any child who will read it. If I was to evaluate it ten out of ten.

By Ashlie Phillipson

I thought *Rupins* was a really good book, and it made me think about how to use my money, and how to make my money last until I need it. I give it 8/10 for my evaluation.

By Sophie H

I thought that *Rupins* was really good. I enjoyed the book and I now know that I can put my money into piles so I can us my money properly. Thank you!!

From Taz Cook

I think *Rupins* is a very interesting book. I really enjoyed reading it. The only thing I thought was not very good was when Will said it's getting late and Ben just agreed. I thought he should of said something more interesting like let's carry on and go home later.

But it was a great book and it has helped me with my money a lot so I would give it 9/10 from Taz Cook.

From Eddy Line

I thought *Rupins* was very, very exciting. I like to thank Miss Cooper for all the work she has done & helped us in Rupins. And I really really enjoyed.

Thank you! Miss Thompson-Wells!

And the bit I enjoyed was when Will and Ben went in the space ship. It was really interesting I wanted to read it over and over again because I want to find out what will happen. Thank you again & Thank you!

Other books by Christine Thompson-Wells:

Will Jones' Space Adventures: The Zadrilian Queen

This follows on from *The Money Formula*. A planet goes into decline with all of its natural resources used up. The inhabitants of the planet no longer see any value in working to maintain a healthy society or planet. When Will visits the Planet Zadril, through the determination of Princess Eex, the people of the planet find new enthusiasm and a desire to achieve something in their lives once again.

See our web page:

www.booksforreadingonline.com

for our other books.

www.ingramcontent.com/pod-product-compliance
Lightning Source LLC
Chambersburg PA
CBHW050832010526
44110CB00054BA/2653